SUPERVISION:
PERSPECTIVES
&
PROPOSITIONS

Prepared by the
ASCD Commission on Supervision Theory

JOHN T. LOVELL, Chairman
Edited by WILLIAM H. LUCIO

Association for Supervision and Curriculum Development, NEA
1201 Sixteenth Street, N.W., Washington, D.C. 20036

Library of Congress Catalog Card Number: 67-29804

Contents

Members of the ASCD Commission on Supervision Theory

John T. Lovell, *Chairman*
Professor of Education, School of Education, Auburn University, Auburn, Alabama

Robert H. Anderson
Professor of Education, Harvard University, Cambridge, Massachusetts

Tom Banahan
Associate Professor of Education, Central Connecticut State College, New Britain, Connecticut

Norman J. Boyan
Associate Professor of Education, School of Education, Stanford University, Stanford, California

Evelyn F. Carlson
Associate Superintendent in Charge of Curriculum Development, Board of Education, Public Schools, Chicago, Illinois

Richard Carlson
Professor of Education, School of Education, University of Oregon, Eugene, Oregon

Arthur Coladarci
Associate Dean, School of Education, Stanford University, Stanford, California

George Gerbner
Professor and Dean, The Annenberg School of Communications, University of Pennsylvania, Philadelphia

John D. Greene
Director of Instruction, Parish School Board, East Baton Rouge, Louisiana

William H. Lucio
Professor of Education, School of Education, University of California, Los Angeles

Lillian Paukner
Executive Director, Department of Elementary Curriculum and Instruction, Public Schools, Milwaukee, Wisconsin

Foreword

OLDER concepts of supervision are as outmoded and imprac-
tical as the "Fish Grabbing with the Bare Hands School" in Benjamin's
Saber Tooth Curriculum. Not only is it not done that way any more, but
it is not even thought about in the same terms. The goals are different,
the forces are better recognized and understood, and the procedures have
changed with this new knowledge. The perspectives and propositions
about supervision in this booklet not only bring the concepts of supervision up-to-date, but provide principles basic to future developments
in this area.

The Board of Directors and Executive Committee are quite con-
scious of the "S" in ASCD. There are times when it seems that supervision
is neglected with the increased attention being given to curriculum development. This booklet, emphasizing as it does the goal-oriented instructional aspects of supervision, the differentiated supervisory functions, and
a team approach to the tasks of supervision, does much to dispel these
fears. Supervision and curriculum development are as intimately related
as we thought they should be.

Practice without a theoretical foundation has been described as trial
and error behavior. Whether or not this is true, the soundest and most
consistent practices are based upon sound theory. There is thus no
apology for the scholarly, well-documented theoretical groundwork in
this bulletin. Also in its favor is a section relating the theory to current
practices. While this booklet does not attempt to present a single, unified
theory of supervision, it does present a thoughtful frame of reference for
analyzing and appraising school supervisory functions.

November 1967   J. HARLAN SHORES, *President*
Association for Supervision
and Curriculum Development

Acknowledgments

FINAL editing of the manuscript and production of this booklet were the responsibility of Robert R. Leeper, Associate Secretary and Editor, ASCD Publications. Technical production was handled by Claire J. Larson, assisted by Mary Ann Lurch, Joan H. Steffenburg and Teola T. Jones.

Preface

A COMMISSION on Supervision Theory was established by the Association for Supervision and Curriculum Development in 1963. This Commission was charged as follows:

To take leadership in the formulation of a theory of supervision based on an analysis of the research in leadership, communication, community power structure, decision making, the process of change, and other relevant areas. It is hoped that the Commission will accept the responsibility for planning and conducting seminars or institutes or other appropriate activities centered around an exploration of segments of research statements and interpretations that are important in evolving a theory of supervision.

The Commission makes no claim that the reports in this publication constitute either a theory of supervision or a definitive position on instructional supervision. It does hope, however, that the concepts and formulations which are presented will serve as a frame of reference for analyzing instructional supervisory behavior in educational institutions and that the ideas presented will generate thinking, discussion, research, and theory development.

A Commission publication is an outgrowth of the productive thinking of a number of persons. Reports and studies were prepared by Commission members at various times and all members participated in discussions. However, not all Commission members chose to present final written statements. Commission members, during their deliberations, developed an openness that made it possible to deal with ideas and problems at a highly realistic level. I hope the results are worthy, and I know that the work with the Commission has greatly enriched my professional experience. Grateful acknowledgement is due those individuals who have served as members of the Commission.

November 1967

JOHN T. LOVELL
Chairman
ASCD Commission
on Supervision Theory

Introduction

THE selections in this publication reflect, in part, the deliberations of the Commission on Supervision Theory during its tenure. These selections also attempt to account for the views of all Commission members as well as to present the positions of the several individual contributors. No attempt is made to claim for the reports a unity which it is obvious they do not possess nor to propose any single theory of supervision. One reason for compiling the work of individual Commission members is simply that it makes these statements more accessible and permanent and thus open for the reactions of others.

Though each section focuses on a particular aspect of supervision, there are several recurrent themes:

1. Recognition of the goal-setting and goal-accomplishing function of supervision

2. An awareness of the instructional aspects of supervision and the requirements of supervisory expertise

3. A concern with the collegial or team approach to defining and accomplishing supervisory tasks

4. A perception of supervision as a differentiated function varying in accordance with the requirements of unique situations.

A brief outline of the contents of the four sections follows: Section I, The Supervisory Function: Overview, Analysis, Propositions, deals with concepts of organization which have affected supervisory purposes and practices; it suggests possible directions for supervisory thought.

Section II, A Perspective for Viewing Instructional Supervisory Behavior, considers a number of organizational variables affecting supervision and presents schemata for viewing instructional supervision in schools.

Section III, Supervision as Teaching: An Analogue, analyzes some of the elements in supervision and defines and describes, in particular, the teaching aspects of supervision.

Section IV, Implications for Educational Practice, draws implications for practice from propositions advanced in other sections and provides examples of supervisory programs.

Each of the sections is intended to present certain points of view and propositions which may be tested in practice. The reader may find the materials useful in developing hypotheses about supervision, formulating appropriate criteria for assessing the supervisory function, and considering new ways of analyzing the situations in which he works. If the report does nothing more than provoke further critical thought about supervision, it will have accomplished its purpose.

November 1967   WILLIAM H. LUCIO

The Supervisory Function: Overview, Analysis, Propositions

William H. Lucio

THE supervisory function has been employed in various forms since man's first attempts to combine individual efforts toward achieving some common end. Actions such as planning, directing, and evaluating the efforts of men or their production (in both informal and formal organizations) in the light of purposes have traditionally constituted supervision. The character of supervision has been influenced in large part by overall organizational strategies, schemes, or doctrines.[1]

In some measure the stability and effectiveness of organizations, whether they be armies, governments, or religious groups, have been dependent upon the kind and quality of supervision. The ways in which organizations have met changing conditions, the degrees of freedom allowed for individual action, the ways in which human potentialities have been utilized, or the evaluation and reward system utilized—all have been parameters affecting organizational health and perpetuation. The effects of organizational behavior may be analyzed from examples such as direction and control of the waterways of early Egypt, or somewhat more recently in history, Hitler's authoritarian decisions vis-à-vis the German armies before the gates of Stalingrad.

As societies and organizations have increased in complexity, the relationships of persons in them have been affected, and the administrative arrangements to facilitate favorable relationships have become complex. The competencies required for effective supervisory behavior have likewise become more complex. Though numerous studies have reported

---

[1] Albert Lepawski. *Administration: The Art and Science of Organization and Management.* New York: Alfred A. Knopf, Inc., 1962. (Chapter 4, pp. 77-106, contains a definitive summary of the historical development of organizations.)

J. Bronowski and Bruce Mazlish. *The Western Intellectual Tradition.* New York and Evanston: Harper Torch Books, Harper & Row Publishers, Inc., 1962.

findings regarding the requisite skills, knowledge, and attitudes needed to achieve individual effectiveness and satisfaction in organizations, many of the provocative results of such studies have yet to be tested in school settings.[2]

Concepts of supervisory functions and practices, borrowed at times from other organizations, have been based on objectives often at variance with the unique purposes of schools; and the uncritical acceptance and application of various administrative "theories" or taxonomies have sometimes resulted in questionable supervisory policies and practices.[3] At times we may have given too little attention to the idea that "the main task of supervision has always been that of the school itself: furtherance of that knowledge by which human beings can comprehend if not control their world."[4]

The various kinds and degrees of titles which have been applied to supervisory personnel (consultant, coordinator, teacher consultant, curriculum assistant, program specialist, director, and similar) seem to reflect a need for more consensus about functional definitions of supervision. Episodes in which supervisory personnel or supervisory departments have been completely eliminated, or their functions assigned to other segments of the school organization are not uncommon. The verbal reasons given for such actions range from statements of "costs" to quasi-philosophical positions. When these episodes are carefully studied, however, one is led to conclude that in many instances the elimination of supervisory services resulted from inadequate formulation of the supervisory task and the absence of visible evidence that the supervisory service was accomplishing its instructional purposes. Ineffective programs of supervision consequently may create a hiatus between schools' objectives and their implementation.

An analysis of some of the theories of management and the ways in which they have influenced supervisory policies and practices in schools [5]

---

[2] Rensis Likert. *New Patterns of Management.* New York: McGraw-Hill Book Company, Inc., 1961.

James G. March, editor. *Handbook of Organizations.* Chicago: Rand McNally & Company, 1965.

[3] Harold Koontz. "Making Sense of Management Theory." *Harvard Business Review* 40:24-46; July-August 1962.

[4] William H. Lucio and John D. McNeil. *Supervision: A Synthesis of Thought and Action.* New York: McGraw-Hill Book Company, Inc., 1962. p. 12.

[5] Scholarly analyses of the pros and cons of scientific management, human relations, and the revisionists are presented in: Warren Bennis. "Revisionist Theory of Leadership." *Harvard Business Review* 39:26-38; January-February 1961.

Amitai Etzioni. *Modern Organizations.* Englewood Cliffs, New Jersey: Prentice-Hall, Inc., 1964.

may serve to explain "how the present came to be" and suggest propositions for examination and testing by supervisors faced with operational planning.

Scientific Management

One of the first comprehensive approaches to the management of organizational life was generated by the writings of Max Weber, Frederick Taylor, and Henri Fayol.[6] Spurred by a desire to increase industrial efficiency through improved management practice, these men viewed organizations as if they existed without people. A coldly scientific appraisal of organizational life was the order of the day, and such was the influence of this school of thought upon industrial management that it eventually came to be labeled as the School of Scientific Management. So widespread was its effect that its tenets dominated administrative thought internationally for a quarter of a century (1910-1935).

An enthusiasm for scientific advance in the field of engineering formed a partial basis for the management movement. The intention of writers in the field was to develop a system of abstract depersonalization that would afford a dependable mechanism to supply solutions leading to greater industrial efficiency without the involvement of human emotion and error. It was Max Weber, a German sociologist, who contributed a theory of administration which provided support for the new movement. Using the word "bureaucracy" to mean what we now refer to as large-scale formal organizations, he suggested that the organization should be built like a vending machine into which industrial problems could be inserted and which would then mechanically disgorge the solutions together with valid reasons for them which were derived from a carefully prepared code.

Frederick Taylor, writing about the same time as Weber, was perhaps more responsible than any other individual for the professionalization of management. Where Weber had stressed the idea of "role" or "position"

[6] Amitai Etzioni, *ibid.*, Chapter 2.
  Richard Bendix. *Max Weber: An Intellectual Portrait.* New York: Doubleday & Company, Inc., 1960.
  Henri Fayol. *General and Industrial Management.* London: Sir Isaac Pitman and Sons, 1949.
  Lucio and McNeil, *op. cit.*, Chapter 1.
  National Society for the Study of Education. *Behavioral Science and Educational Administration.* Sixty-third Yearbook. Chicago: the Society, 1964. Chapter III.
  Frederick W. Taylor. *Scientific Management.* New York: Harper and Brothers, 1947.

in a hierarchy, Taylor stressed the impersonal rationality of measurement. It was this impersonal mathematical approach that caused Taylor to become labeled as "the Father of Scientific Management." Taylor's theory combines a study of physical capabilities of a worker with an economic approach which views man as driven by the fear of hunger and the search for profit. The basic theme underlying Taylor's thought seems to be that if material rewards are closely related to work efforts, the worker will respond with the maximum performance of which he is physically capable. Taylor, it would appear, viewed human endeavor as simply a mechanical addition to the industrial complex of his time.

Henri Fayol was Taylor's counterpart in France. Fayol believed, as did Taylor, that the problem of personnel and its management was the key to industrial success at all levels. He proposed a clearly defined "chain of command" with rigid channels of communication and advocated the selection of the proper person for each specific job as being of prime importance to management.

The revolution in management perspective generated by the ideas of Weber, Taylor, and Fayol influenced not only practices in industrial organizations but practices in schools as well. Administrators adopted the tenets of the movement and supervisory practices reflected this perspective of employee position and worth.[7]

Thus the supervisory function in the first quarter of the century was dominated by a "classical view" of man and institutions. Teachers were to be closely directed and required to carry out practices determined by administrative personnel. Teachers were to be held to certain standards of performance and rated accordingly. Influenced by the scientific management theories with their emphasis on product, measurement, and testing, the attainment of set standards by pupils and teachers became the rule. Thus, an important purpose of supervision was to discover laws of teaching and learning and to require teachers to apply these laws under direction.[8] The supervisory function was viewed as a kind of "pipeline" model whereby ideas in supervisors' minds trickled down to teachers who were to act as implementers or "huskers." Assumptions undergirding "scientific supervision" included views that schools were staffed by persons who had to be led because they did not know what they were doing, that it was useless to look to teachers for sources of new ideas, that administrative levels of supervision were the central sources of knowledge, and that the problems of schools were known, but known to only a few select individuals.

[7] Raymond E. Callahan. *Education and the Cult of Efficiency.* Chicago: The University of Chicago Press, 1962.

[8] Lucio and McNeil, *op. cit.,* Chapter I.

Though many aspects of the scientific management movement were perceived as "inhuman," reactions stimulated in part by the way Taylor stated his beliefs about human beings, nevertheless a number of ideas from the movement still have currency. For example, organizational policies and practices continue to be affected by, and give consideration to, the function of goal setting, the systematic definition of tasks, the measurement of performance and output, the design of physical work space, and the idea of separating the planning function from the performing function. Current curriculum strategies involving task analysis, sequential programming, and assessment of performance may be reflections of the movement. In general, however, the scientific management movement created unfavorable repercussions in government and labor circles, and with the emergence of new interpretations of organizational life the popularity of the movement eventually declined.

Human Relations

By the mid-1930's the reaction to scientific management, supported in part by the Western Electric studies, dealt a crushing blow to the economically motivated model of man. Attention was focused on human relations processes, on new ways of influencing personnel toward change, or on new solutions to the age-old problem of man versus organizations.

About 1935 the results of the work done by Mayo, Roethlisberger, and their associates became prominent.[9] Mayo, working at the Hawthorne Plant of the Western Electric Company, devised a series of experiments the results of which seemed seriously to contradict the tenets and principles of the Scientific Management theorists. Mayo concluded that production output was closely related to the social satisfaction of the individual worker. A further conclusion seemed to be that the major problems of management are found in the realm of human relations, rather than in technical processes. Employees, it was claimed, had to be viewed as individuals with psychological drives and social needs rather than simply as mass appendages to an industrial machine.

The new stress on the human element in industry caused the Mayo

[9] Elton Mayo. "The Fruitful Errors of Elton Mayo." *Fortune Magazine* 34(5):181-251; November 1964.

Elton Mayo. *The Human Problems of an Industrial Civilization.* Boston: Harvard Business School, 1933.

Elton Mayo. *The Social Problems of an Industrial Civilization.* Boston: Harvard Business School, 1945.

Fritz J. Roethlisberger and William J. Dickson. *Management and The Worker.* Cambridge, Massachusetts: Harvard University Press, 1939.

approach to be known as the Human Relationist School. The major assumption was that man could be motivated to more productive work by helping him fulfill his social and psychological needs rather than by simply furnishing him adequate pay.

Essential to the Human Relations approach is the recognition of the existence of informal groups within the formal organizational structure. Applying Kurt Lewin's concept that the group to which an individual belongs is the ground for his perceptions, his feelings, and his actions, the human relationists pointed out that it is through the informal group that the social need-satisfaction is provided. The rash of company-sponsored bowling and baseball teams, company picnics, and company recreational facilities provided by industry during the 1930-40 period can be traced directly to the human relationist influence, since the human relationist model does not recognize any conflict between organizational objectives and the provision of such facilities. Satisfying the workers' social and psychological needs is entirely congruent with the organization's goals of effectiveness and productivity.

Subsequent experience and research have pointed out, however, that high morale does not guarantee high productivity. Serious questions concerning the basic assumptions of the Human Relationist perspective began to be asked, so that by 1950 theorists were seeking a new approach that would provide the advantages of both the Scientific and the Human Relationist schools.

Findings and propositions of the human relations movement strongly influenced supervisory policies and practices in schools, and much attention was given to human relations processes as a way of influencing personnel toward instructional change. Equalitarian and personalized supervisory approaches were utilized to direct teachers toward the goals of the school. Supervisors accepted observational methods from other fields.

Classroom situations were often evaluated as through the eyes of a psychoanalyst. Value judgments about teaching were common ("the teacher is warm and friendly"), judgments which frequently bore little relation to the goals of schooling or to teacher performance in changing pupil behavior. As a result, supervision tended to analyze the *incidentals* rather than the *consequences* of teaching, focused on personal attributes of teachers and pupils, described teacher behavior in terms of *inference* rather than in terms of *observed* effects on pupils, and tended to view effective teachers as those whose performance was *congruent* with some *hypothetical model*.

In schools the application of rational thought in problem solving began to receive less emphasis; and the organizational goals were de-emphasized in favor of individual and group purposes—purposes the achievement of which may have contributed little to the worthy goals of teaching or to the organizational integrity of the school. At times, supervision gave attention or loyalty to various external tasks, often of a "clerical" nature, and not always related to teaching-learning problems. When emphasis was placed on peripheral functions, the result was to neglect, if not to abrogate, responsibility for furthering the goals of the school and the knowledge and skills by which persons can comprehend and control the real world.[10]

Leavitt reexamined the human relations participative beliefs, and suggested that differentiated approaches to task accomplishment might be more appropriate than single, all-inclusive strategies (e.g., scientific management) applied uniformly anywhere and everywhere in an organization. His views reflect a transition in thought to the discussion of the revisionist position:

In asking for a second look at the participative beliefs, I have tried not to associate myself with some others who are asking for the same thing but for quite different reasons.

. . . I am not worried about "manipulation," "group-think," "softness," "conformity," or any of the other recent criticisms. In fact, most theories and techniques of human relations are, to my mind, both sound and progressive. *The theme here is not that human relations theory is either incorrect or immoral. My argument is that it is simply insufficient. It is too narrow a perspective from which to analyze the management of organizations.* But I am not suggesting that we turn back to the earlier and even narrower beliefs of "tough" management. What we have to do is to push beyond the plateau of present beliefs . . .

. . . Nor am I worried about groups replacing individuals. In my opinion the participative beliefs represent a great advance in management, one that needs now only to be placed in perspective.

In our eagerness over the last couple of decades to expand and test our new and exciting findings about participation, we may have made two serious but understandable and correctable mistakes: we have on occasion confused our observations with our values; and we have assumed that our participative beliefs represented the absolute zero of management—that there was no more basic level.

But though I believe in the values associated with the participative beliefs and in their great practical utility for solving huge present and future problems of human relationships, I ask that we try to fit them into the still broader perspective on organizations that is being generated out of the communication and systems sciences, and out of our rapidly growing understanding of the processes of thinking, organizing, and problem solving.

[10] Lucio and McNeil, *op. cit.*, Chapter I.

One way of setting these beliefs into a different perspective may be, I submit, by viewing large organizations as differentiated sets of subsystems rather than as unified wholes. Such a view leads us toward a management-by-task kind of outlook—with the recognition that many subparts of the organization may perform many different kinds of tasks, and therefore, may call for many different kinds of managerial practices.[11]

The Revisionists

Since 1950, a number of authors have attempted to reconcile the Scientific Management and the Human Relationist viewpoints. These theorists are generally referred to as the Revisionists or Structuralists. Their hope and intent is to eliminate the unrealistic aspects of the Human Relationist approach without sacrificing the advantages of its departures from the viewpoint of Scientific Management.

In combining the positive values of the mechanists who emphasized the organizational goals, and those of the Human Relationists who emphasized the social goals of individuals, the Revisionists attempt to consider both individual and organizational goals in their proper perspective. They recognize that the individual goals and the organizational goals must be fused through commitment and leadership activity; and they hold the view that external economic factors must be considered along with productivity and formal status, but not to the exclusion of the human elements that the Scientific theorists neglected. The Revisionists hold that work is a natural activity of men, that the goals of the organization can be used as incentives to intelligent work, that lack of control is undesirable in any organization, and that employee participation in decision making is harmonious with the accountability assumed by administrators.

Among the Revisionists, the studies of Argyris and McGregor are representative, although the earlier work of Barnard was also germinal.[12]

[11] Harold J. Leavitt. "Unhuman Organizations." *Harvard Business Review* 40:90-98; July-August 1962.

[12] Chris Argyris. *Executive Leadership.* New York: Harper and Brothers, 1953.

Chris Argyris. *Interpersonal Competence and Organizational Effectiveness.* Homewood, Illinois: Irwin-Dorsey Press, 1962.

Chris Argyris. *Personality and Organization.* New York: Harper and Brothers, 1957.

E. Wight Bakke. *The Fusion Process.* New Haven, Connecticut: Labor and Management Center, Yale University, 1953.

Chester I. Barnard. *The Functions of the Executive.* Cambridge, Massachusetts: Harvard University Press, 1950.

Douglas M. McGregor. *The Human Side of Enterprise.* New York: McGraw-Hill Book Company, Inc., 1960.

Argyris deals directly with the man-organization problem by stating quite succinctly that individual needs and formal organization demands are basically incompatible. His solution is to provide the possibility of self-actualization for the employee through (a) job enlargement, and (b) employee-centered leadership as a modification of directive leadership. The resolution of the conflict involves improving the diagnostic skills of management and making use of the talents of staff specialists to help the organization attain these skills—a fusion designed to bring about the greatest actualization of both organization and the individual.

McGregor assessed the man-organization problem as that of an inherent tension which results from conflict between individual needs and organizational demands and developed two sets of assumptions under the rubrics of Theory X and Theory Y. Theory X defines a traditional, authoritarian, or controlled view of the problem (persons dislike work, do not accept responsibility, and have to be controlled, directed, rewarded, or punished); while Theory Y describes a more participative or permissive view (persons like work, will use self-direction in meeting organizational objectives, and will express creative thought in solving problems). McGregor affirmed that the propositions in Theory Y pointed to a more realistic way of examining the nature and functioning of present-day organizations. He posited that systematic application of these propositions to organizational problems (through rational participative action) would result in better integration of man and organization.

In general, Revisionist proposals have suggested provocative ways of designing organizational life. A more balanced perspective of school supervision may result from the application of Revisionist suggestions concerning individual and institutional purposes and needs.[13] Unitary emphasis on the purposes and demands of either the school or the individual would be "deweighted" but neither would be "devalued" at the expense of the other. The work of various researchers [14] indicates that

13 See: William H. Read. "The Decline of the Hierarchy in Industrial Organizations."; and Thomas R. Brooks. "Can Employees 'Manage' Themselves?" Both articles reprinted in issues of A Notes and Quotes Reprint, 1965. (Published by Connecticut General Life Insurance Company, Hartford, Connecticut.)

Bennis, loc. cit.

Lucio and McNeil, loc. cit.

McGregor, op. cit., pp. 1-58; 110-23.

14 Chris Argyris. "A New Era in Personnel Relations." Dun's Review and Modern Industry 79(6):40-41, 171-78. June 1962.

Leavitt, loc. cit.

Likert, loc. cit.

Herbert A. Simon. Administrative Behavior. New York: The Macmillan Company, 1957.

the search for theoretical approaches to ways of integrating the task-serving and needs-serving purposes of organizations continues.

In light of experience it would seem that the supervisory function should be defined not in terms of any one single doctrine or comprehensive, normative theory but in terms of various situational parameters in schools. Efforts should be addressed to defining better the purposes of schooling, the relation and application of individual talent to tasks, and the consequences of methods applied to particular problems and situations.[15]

Among the current conditions inviting new approaches to work systems in schools are: (a) the specialization of knowledge requiring more teacher-supervisor expertise, (b) the national demands for the improved preparation of teachers and supervisors, (c) the stimulus to curriculum change generated by various learned societies and research centers, and (d) new technologies and teaching strategies.[16]

If a working society of professional co-equals most proximate to the teaching function can be established, then the older hierarchical lines of demarcation between the "leader" and the "led" become less important; traditional vertical relationships of supervisor-subordinate are de-emphasized. Because of the differentiated nature of learning tasks in schools and concomitant needs for varied human talents, vertical lines of authority in schools may no longer represent an appropriate distribution of talent and intellect. More and more, talent is where one finds it. Increasingly, teachers and supervisors will establish lateral working relationships with one another,[17] and by re-planning their ways of working, develop non-hierarchical, collegial, team strategies to tackle the problems facing schools in our society.

Summary Propositions

New ways of viewing organizational functioning, including the decentralization and realignment of decision-making processes, increased professional accountability for determining educational goals, planning

[15] Amitai Etzioni. "Two Approaches to Organizational Analysis: A Critique and a Suggestion." *Administrative Science Quarterly* 5:261; September 1960.

Raymond A. Katzell. "Contrasting Systems of Work Organization." *American Psychologist* 17:107; February 1962.

Herbert H. Meyer; Emanuel Kay, and John R. P. French, Jr. "Split Roles in Performance Appraisal." *Harvard Business Review* 43(1):123-29; January-February 1965.

[16] See articles under the heading: "Changing Directions in American Education." *Saturday Review* 50(2):37; January 14, 1967.

[17] Read, *loc. cit.*

teaching strategies, and the assessment of learning outcomes, suggest the following directions for supervision:

1. *Supervision by objectives.* The mutual concern of all professionals involved in schooling is directed toward the rational accomplishment of defined objectives and tasks—individual and organizational needs are closely meshed.

2. *Teacher-supervisor joint responsibility.* Emphasis is upon development of skills for ferreting out current knowledge and testing its application to unique situations, with the focus on acquiring theories, knowledge, and skills throughout the professional life-span. The enhancement of teaching as "an organizational career" thus upgrades the profession.

3. *Differentiated supervision.* Supervision is differentiated according to the behavior required of persons in various positions in schools. Holding professional trust and competence constant, the question of placing the supervisory function becomes a relative matter. The supervisory function operates whenever decisions among alternative objectives are made, strategies to achieve defined purposes are planned, and results are explicitly evaluated.

A Perspective for Viewing Instructional Supervisory Behavior

John T. Lovell

THAT supervisory behavior exists in schools and is in a constant process of change as a result of a complex set of interdependent factors is clear. The question is not whether there will be instructional supervisory behavior but whether the nature of this behavior can be controlled in such a way that student learning will be influenced in certain specified ways. In order to achieve such a condition, it will be necessary to develop a "system" of concepts by which to view the phenomenon of "instructional supervisory behavior." The purpose in this section is to develop such a framework and to derive a definition of the function of instructional supervisory behavior in achieving and maintaining organizational goals.

The Conceptual Framework

In the system of concepts presented in this paper, the institution of education is defined as a "subsystem" of society. Society is seen as specifying the "function" and terminal goals of schooling; that is, the facilitation of student learning in certain operationally defined directions assumed to be congruent with society's expectation. The basic function for achieving this goal is defined as the "teaching function." The teacher, operating from a unique frame of reference, develops certain procedures which, it is hypothesized, will result in certain pupil learnings. Such operational units constitute "teacher-pupil systems" whose outputs are defined in terms of pupil behavior; and such outputs are seen as inputs for the organization.

Instructional supervisory behavior, while external to the teacher-pupil system, is calculated to influence directly and purposefully teacher behavior in such a way as to facilitate student learning. A view of supervisory behavior within the context of the organizational structure, as seen from this frame of reference, is presented in Figure 1. (Page 14.)

The school is thus seen as being made up of a large number of interdependent supersystems, systems, and subsystems, with interdependent, interacting, and organized variables and/or elements in some specified educational unit. For example, the teacher working with a group of children is an "educational social system" and is seen as a subsystem of the teacher-pupil system. Obviously, more than one teacher-pupil system exists within a particular school. These teacher-pupil systems also constitute their own system. Instructional supervisory behavior, as a part of the external environment of the teacher-pupil systems, and interacting with teacher behavior, constitutes another subsystem. The goal of this subsystem is to facilitate the achievement of the goals of the teacher-pupil system. When instructional supervisory behavior is defined in this way, it has many dimensions.

Teachers, supervisors, superintendents, or principals who participate in a kind of behavior officially designated by the organization and directly affecting the teacher and/or the teacher-pupil system are serving in an instructional supervisory capacity. That this is the only behavior which influences teacher behavior is not implied. On the contrary, there is a most significant "informal behavior system" which also changes teacher behavior. It is not the purpose of this paper to deal with this aspect of behavior unless implications for supervision are apparent.

Functions for Facilitating Teaching

The reasons why organizations find it necessary to provide for officially designated functions by which to facilitate teaching behavior are varied. A discussion of six possible ways follows.[1]

Goal Development

If instructional supervisory behavior is to meet certain organizational needs, the functions of such behavior may be better understood by an examination of the nature of the organization. Basically, organizations represent a patterning of specialized and interdependent parts which human beings create to achieve some common goal or goals. Since teacher-pupil systems are subsystems of larger systems such as the local school (with goals which are subgoals of the overall goals of the local system), ideally, therefore, teachers, because of their expertise, should

---

[1] The author was significantly influenced by the writings of Likert, Argyris, Barnard, and Herzberg in the development of these functions.

Figure 1. Supervisory Behavior: A Conceptual Framework

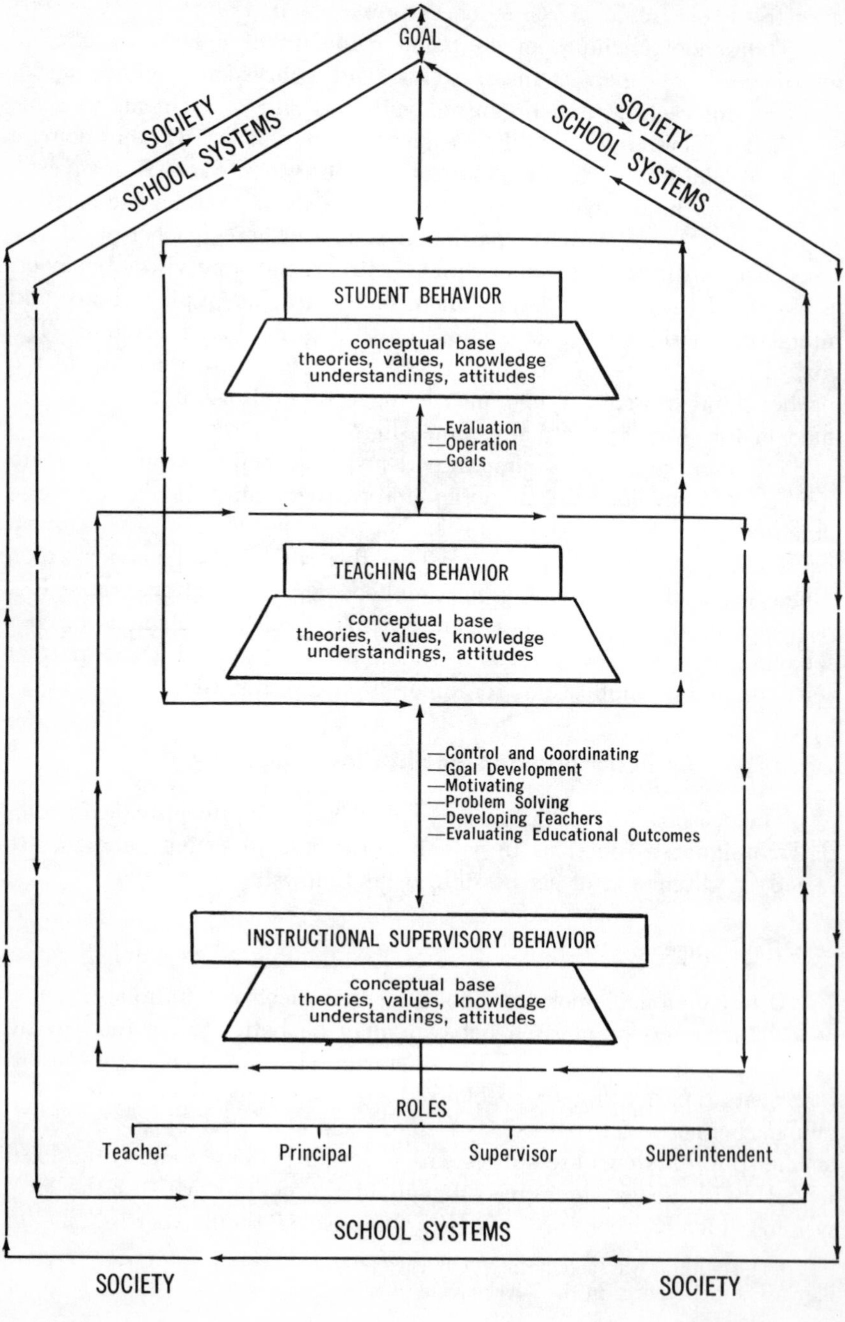

be participants in a coordinated effort to develop operational goals of teacher-pupil systems that will be congruent with those of local schools, school districts, and super systems such as society.

Control and Coordination

The second function of instructional supervisory behavior is conceptualized as coordination and control of those unique or specialized features of an organization.

Motivation

According to Barnard, a necessary condition for the existence of any organization is a willingness on the part of organizational members to work for the attainment of the organizational goals.[2] Educational organizations must make provisions for the motivation of the teaching staff to assure the achievement of educational goals.

Professional Development

Organizational workers (teachers) are highly trained professionals, having attained a high level of competence in certain conceptual, human, and technical skills. Nevertheless, the skills needed in teaching in a modern technological society are rapidly changing and require the continuous development of teachers in such a way as to ensure behavior appropriate for the achievement of organizational goals.

Problem Solving

When teaching is conceptualized as goal identification, development of operations for achieving goals, and evaluation of goal achievement, human problem solving is the central activity in teacher-pupil systems.

Evaluation of Educational Outcomes

Since educational organizations have goals and use resources for achieving goals, it is essential to provide a systematic procedure for the evaluation of the output of the educational social system. Teaching has been defined as the basic function for achieving the goals of the educational organization. Therefore, evaluation of the learning outcomes of

[2] Chester I. Barnard. *The Functions of the Executive.* Cambridge, Massachusetts: Harvard University Press, 1938. p. 72.

teacher-pupil systems is identified as the sixth function of instructional supervisory behavior.

Sources of Supervisory Behavior

Viewing the conceptual scheme just presented, several factors stand out as important determinants of the function of the supervisory behavior system. First, it is apparent that the basic work of the institution (teaching) is done by teachers. What assumptions are made about teachers? Are they professionally competent specialists or are they passive instruments of administration who carry out relatively mundane tasks designed and developed at a "higher" theoretical level? Perceiving the teacher as a creative, self-directing, and responsible decision maker and problem solver, has implications for defining instructional supervisory behavior.

Second, the conceptual scheme clearly indicates that instructional supervisory behavior seeks to influence the teacher-pupil behavior system, and, therefore, the nature of this behavior is at least partly a function of the conceptualization of teaching. Teaching may be conceptualized as a creative response to an emerging situation by a professionally competent specialist, or, on the other hand, as the achievement of a specialized task by a technician.

Third, since supervisory behavior always occurs within the framework of a "social system," it is partly a function of the social system in which it operates. Social systems are characterized by boundary, tension and conflict, disequilibration—re-equilibration, and feedback. The nature of supervisory behavior is limited by the limitation of the social system in which it occurs. Efforts to change the nature of supervisory behavior in educational organizations without changing the organizational structure might well prove futile.

So far, the following factors have been identified as sources from which instructional supervisory behavior derives its distinctive features:

1. The characteristics of human beings in schools
2. The nature of the "social systems" in which instructional supervisory behavior occurs
3. The nature of teaching and learning
4. The organizational structure of schools.

The Characteristics of Human Beings in Schools

March and Simon have grouped propositions about human behavior in organizations in three broad classes as follows:

1. Organization members, and particularly employees, are primarily passive instruments, capable of performing work and accepting directions, but not of initiating action or exerting influence in any significant way.

2. Members bring to their organizations attitudes, values, and goals; they have to be motivated or induced to participate in the system of organizational behavior; there is incomplete parallelism between their personal goals and organization goals; and actual or potential goal conflicts make power phenomena, attitudes, and morale centrally important in the explanation of organizational behavior.

3. Organization members are decision makers and problem solvers, and perception and thought processes are central to the explanation of behavior in organizations.[3]

Most authorities would agree with the description of man as a rational and emotional goal-seeking organism. However, is man capable of self-determination of direction? Is the nature of human beings in educational institutions such that external sources of control (hierarchy) are needed to direct (goal determination) and motivate man to participate in behavior which will ensure the achievement of organizational goals? Or, are men in educational institutions capable of self-direction, goal setting, problem solving, and rational decision making? These propositions do not suggest complete individual freedom or autonomy. Obviously, man must live within the social framework of the organization. Earl Kelley expressed this thought as follows:

The basic, organismic demand for freedom is, in one sense, limited and curtailed by the equally powerful need to be social. Man needs freedom and he also needs other people. Therefore, these two needs have to be reconciled. No human being can exercise complete freedom to do as he pleases and retain his status with his fellows. He would soon be alone, deprived of one of the most important stuffs of growth, and in this solitary condition his development will be warped. This result can be observed in all people who are shut off from social intercourse with their own kind.[4]

The problem is not whether man should be free but whether or not professional members of educational organizations are capable and self-motivating enough to participate in "system" goal setting, problem solving, and rational decision making.

It is expected that the actual work of the institution (teaching) is performed by professionally competent specialists. As a matter of fact, the professional teacher with adequate experience is probably the most

[3] James G. March and Herbert A. Simon. *Organizations*. New York: John Wiley & Sons, Inc., 1961. p. 6.

[4] Earl C. Kelley and Marie I. Rasey. *Education and the Nature of Man*. New York: Harper and Brothers, 1952. p. 103.

competent to teach a particular group of children a particular subject at a particular grade level. This is because the teacher knows the interests, strengths, weaknesses, and special problems of his group. This does not mean he does not need help; he does; but in the final analysis the teacher must be responsible for and have the authority to develop the teaching process.

If the teaching function is important enough to require a high level of professional competence, then it is imperative that teachers be given high status in decision making in the area of curriculum and instruction. Not only are teachers highly specialized but also their specialities are so diffuse that this fact precludes the possibility of "supervision" by general administration on the basis of expertise. Further, the teacher utilizes a broad spectrum of specialities such as subject matter competence, pupil diagnosis, and methodology from which he develops his own expertise. Thus, the possibility of "general monitoring" by an officer of the organization is also precluded.

The teaching role itself is also characterized by teacher specialization rather than task specialization, meaning that teaching is a creative and emerging process in which the teacher is continuously responding in terms of rational analysis to ever-changing situations.

Implications for Instructional Supervisory Behavior: If the teacher is viewed as a dedicated and competent professional, then overseeing or monitoring notions based on either expertise or hierarchical authority would appear to be inappropriate instructional supervisory behavior. Rather, the function would be to initiate and maintain decision-making systems in which the greatest amount of professional competence could be brought to bear on a given decision or problem at a given time. It would be through the initiation and maintenance of such systems that the organization could continuously develop, maintain, and evaluate the operations for achieving organizational goals.

The Nature of the "Social Systems"

Operating from the conceptual framework of system theory, the school has been described as being made up of a large number of loosely related "educational social systems" and instructional supervisory behavior defined as behavior which directly influences teacher-pupil behavior systems. Since supervisory behavior always affects teacher behavior within the context of a social system, it becomes necessary to describe a conceptualization of human problem solving in social systems.

The "system model" used by scientists in the physical sciences, biological sciences, and social sciences provides us with a way of conceptualizing the educational situation in which change occurs in educational institutions. By using the social system model, it is possible to understand the educational social system in terms of boundary, tension, equilibration-disequilibration, and feedback.[5]

Boundaries of the Educational Social System: The way the educational social system is differentiated from the outside environment is the stuff which gives the system a unique identity. In the case of a principal and his staff, it is the job of developing, implementing, and evaluating a school program for a particular group of children. This is a common goal that holds the group together and sets it apart from the outside environment. This does not mean there is no interaction with the outside. External forces which interact with the system are thought of as inputs. The system's influence on the external environment is thought of as the system's output.

Tension, Frustration, and Conflicts: Since individuals in the system are unique, with different purposes and different perceptions of reality, and since there are forces from the outside which constantly feed into the system, tension, frustration, and conflict are inevitable. They tend to distort the system or throw it off balance. It is through the process of human problem solving that the system is able to gain a new equilibrium.

Disequilibration—Re-equilibration: When external or internal forces operate to upset the balance, the system is thrown into a problem-solving situation. This is, of course, an attempt to "re-equilibrate." This does not mean that the system returns to the same state of equilibration as before, but rather that a new state of equilibrium is developed. When the equilibration of the system is upset by internal or external pressure, the system begins to seek to reach a new level of equilibrium. The processes of communication, decision making, leadership, scientific problem solving, and cooperation are used by the system to solve its problem. The way these processes are used determines the effectiveness of the system in developing new states of equilibrium. Some explanation of the operation of these processes might clarify the point.

The process of communication is used to receive, code or decode, evaluate, and transmit information. In the problem-solving situation, the quality of this process is imperative. If the system is transmitting or receiving distorted information, then, such information is used in solving the problem. The quality of communication also affects the creativity of the group process and the kind and degree of innovations

[5] Robert Chin. "The Utility of System Models and Development Models for Practitioners." *The Planning of Change.* Warren G. Bennis, Kenneth D. Benne, and Robert Chin, editors. New York: Holt, Rinehart and Winston, Inc., 1961. pp. 201-14.

for solving problems that result in growth of the ability of the system to solve problems. System members must understand the "reality" of the outside forces that are making an impact on the system. Communications which are distorted and inconsistent lead to internal conflict, tension, and mistrust. Communication inadequacies disturb the process of cooperation in the social system because internal strife causes individuals to lose their ability to cooperate and make adequate decisions.

Feedback in the Educational Social Systems: Recently a rocket ship was put into orbit around the earth's surace, with built-in devices sensitive to the "rocket ship system's" relation to its environment. When certain things actually went wrong and the rocket tilted, this information was fed back into the system and the ship was returned to earth after two rotations instead of the planned three. This is an example of feedback in a system.

The educational social system has been described in terms of boundaries, tension, disequilibration-equilibration, and feedback. But what about change in educational social systems? How and why does it occur? Are men merely victims of a wide variety of social systems of which they are a part or can they control their own destiny? Is the structure of the system set, or can men release clogged-up parts and induce and control change in self-determined directions based on perceived needs and rational choice? It would seem that they can.

Man, operating as a part of a wide variety of social systems, can continuously define and redefine goals and continuously improve his capacity for achieving these goals through the process of planned change. These processes have been identified as leadership, communication, decision making, problem solving, and cooperation. Instructional supervisory behavior can be defined specifically as that organizationally provided behavior that directly and purposefully affects the pupil-teacher systems. This constitutes an external force which is a supervisory behavior system output and teacher-pupil system input, and causes a disequilibration which throws the teacher-pupil system into a problem-solving process in order to achieve a new level of equilibrium. A diagram (see Figure 2) provides a model to illustrate this concept.

Human A, Human B, and Human C make up the social system. These human beings are held together in the system by the assumption that they can achieve certain goals (personal or group) through identification with the group. The system is thus given an identity or boundary which separates it from external systems.

Members of the social system, in working to achieve certain personal and/or group goals, are involved in problem solving resulting in changes which may improve the social system.

PROCESSES OF CHANGE

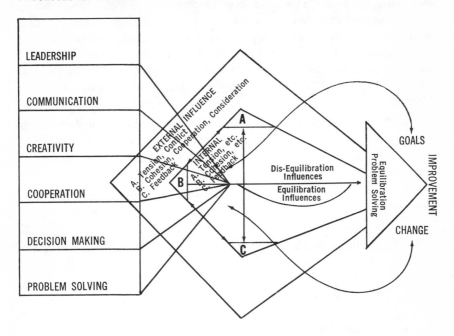

Figure 2. Model for Change in Educational Social Systems

The system's process of change is affected by external forces, i.e., tension, internal conflict, or cohesion; and internal forces, i.e., interpersonal conflicts resulting from personality differences or role conflicts, either or both of which may result in disequilibration which causes the system either to disintegrate or to reach out for a new level of "equilibration" through problem-solving activities.

In this particular model, six processes of change are identified as critical to continuous system improvement—leadership, communication, creativity, decision making, cooperation, and problem solving. These are the processes through which members of the educational social system seek improvement.

Implications for Instructional Supervisory Behavior: The central theme of the theoretical frame of reference just presented is that teacher-pupil systems are the basic structure through which the institution of public education achieves its goals. Human problem solving is defined as determination of goals and values, assumptions about future events, determination of alternative courses of action, selection of desirable action, implementation of the action, evaluation of goal attainment, and evaluation of goals. The basic processes through which human beings solve their problems have been identified as leadership, communication, scientific problem solving, cooperation, creativity, and decision making.

Since human problem solving occurs within the context of organizational subsystems, the nature of instructional supervisory behavior (defined as the facilitation of problem solving) may be summarized as follows:

1. Facilitation of the process of continuous goal identification, teaching, operations development, and evaluation in teacher-pupil systems

2. The development, maintenance, and evaluation of teacher-pupil systems for achieving organizational goals

3. The development, maintenance, and evaluation of the following intra-system and intersystem processes of teacher-pupil systems:

    a. leadership
    b. scientific problem solving
    c. communication
    d. decision making
    e. cooperation
    f. creativity.

4. The coordination of varied teacher-pupil systems in terms of overall organizational instructional goals.

The Nature of Teaching and Learning

Teaching is conceptualized as having three aspects: goal identification, development of operations for achieving goals, and evaluation of goal achievement.

Goal Identification: It has been stated previously that the institution of education is a subsystem of the society of which it is a part, the society specifying both its functions (socialization and extension of knowledge) and terminal goals; and further, that teacher-pupil systems are subsystems of a "local school" which is a subsystem of a school district. This means that the operational goals of a particular teacher-pupil system are interdependent with other teacher-pupil systems in the process of achieving the overall goals of the particular local school. Therefore, the teacher cannot act as an autonomous unit in developing operational goals for his particular teaching unit. Rather, the task of goal development must be coordinated in such a way as to assure that each specialized unit will contribute to the achievement of overall system goals.

Development of Operations for Achieving Goals: Even though teachers are assumed to be professionally competent, they cannot be specialists in all of the sources of knowledge which have implications for teaching. The structure and methodology of the basic organized disciplines, therefore, have strong implications for teaching.

Because of the rapid expansion of knowledge in (a) educational technology, (b) behavioral sciences, (c) curriculum development, (d) teaching and learning resources, and (e) educational research, teachers need specialized assistance.

The important point is that teachers have the responsibility and, therefore, must have the authority for determining teaching operation which it is assumed will achieve certain operationally defined objectives. However, the complexity of the task of developing teaching operations is recognized and, therefore, so is the need for specialized assistance for teachers. It is assumed that as professionals, teachers will utilize such resources.

Evaluation: It is also recognized that the process of evaluation cannot be left to the individual teacher. Rather, systematic evaluation must be developed in such a way as to determine the effectiveness of the teacher-pupil subsystems in terms of the overall goals of the school.

Implications for Instructional Supervisory Behavior: The function of instructional supervisory behavior in providing specialized assistance is as follows:

1. To provide a source of expert information, knowledge, theoretical formulations, and skills from the organized disciplines to enrich the content in the instructional program, and to determine implications for teaching methodology.

2. To provide for the initiation, maintenance, and evaluation of supervisory subsystems in which professionally competent humans with a wide range of appropriate specialities are brought together to develop decision policies and to serve as a resource to teachers in the creation, development, and scientific evaluation of teaching.

The Organizational Structure

Since the supervisory behavior system is a subsystem of the organization, it follows that the organizational structure defines, and controls to some extent, the nature of supervisory behavior. Thus, it would appear to be futile to attempt to study supervisory behavior without a study of the organization in which it occurs. Basically, organizations represent a patterning of specialized and interdependent parts created to achieve some common goal or goals.

There is an educational hierarchy which determines authority and responsibility in developing, implementing, and evaluating policies. There are organizational expectations and general rules which have an impact on human behavior in the organization, and at the same time there are incongruences between individual needs and organizational expectations. It is not the purpose here to analyze these factors; the purpose is to recognize them. If we want human beings with special competence in curriculum and instruction to influence the instructional program in educational organizations, then we must recognize, utilize, and modify the nature of the organizational structure within which instructional supervisory behavior occurs. Instead of ignoring or opposing legitimate authority, why not use legitimate organizational authority to facilitate the work of professionally competent individuals who participate in instructional supervisory behavior?

When there is a lack of congruence between the organizational structure and the needs of the organization, two possible avenues of improvement are available. First, change the needs of the organization; second, change the nature of the organization so that it is more compatible with needs. Certainly, in the case of the educational organization it is possible and desirable to do the latter. This requires continuous and comprehensive analysis and evaluation utilizing the best available "conceptual tools."

Implications for Instructional Supervisory Behavior: The organizational structure of institutions of public education has the following implications for instructional supervisory behavior:

1. To recognize and utilize the organizational structure to influence teachers and teacher-pupil systems in order to facilitate the achievement of educational goals.

2. To seek to modify the organizational structure in such a way as to facilitate the maintenance of human beings in the organization, the maintenance of the organization, and the achievement of organizational goals.

Summary

Instructional supervisory behavior, defined as organizational behavior external to the teacher-pupil system but calculated to impact directly and purposefully on teacher behavior, was defined as having the following functions in educational organizations:

1. Goal development

2. Coordination and control
3. Motivation
4. Problem solving
5. Professional development
6. Evaluation.

The conceptual scheme has proposed the following factors as important determinants of the distinctive features of instructional supervisory behavior as it functions in educational institutions:

1. The characteristics of human beings in the institution of public education

2. The nature of teaching and learning

3. The nature of the "social system" in the institutions of public education in which instructional supervisory behavior occurs

4. The organizational structure of institutions of public education.

Careful study of these four factors made it possible to define the nature of instructional supervisory behavior as follows:

1. *The goal development function:* Teachers are highly trained and specialized professionals. It is important that their expertise be utilized in the critical process of goal development and goal evaluation. It is also essential that teachers be aware of and identified with the overall goals of the organization. One of the most effective ways to provide for this is through the process of teacher involvement in the goal development function.

2. *The coordinating and controlling function:* The description of the teacher as a dedicated competent professional gives cause to question traditional notions of supervisory behavior, which is required to control and coordinate teaching behavior. For example, overseeing or monitoring notions based on either expertise or hierarchical authority might well be inappropriate behavior. Rather, instructional supervisory behavior would be provided by the organization to initiate and maintain decision-making systems in which the greatest amount of professional competence could be brought to bear in the continuous process of developing and maintaining the social structure which would provide the necessary behavior controls.

The description of the organization as a social system with a large number of interdependent subsystems moving toward a common goal clearly establishes the need for coordination and control. Controls must be provided to maintain common direction and systematic evaluation to ascertain the extent to which goals are being achieved. But the description of teachers as professionals indicates that the source of authority for the social structure should be the teachers and administrators themselves.

3. *The motivating function:* Both the discussions of teaching and organizations indicate the necessity of a high level of teacher motivation for an "effective" and "efficient" organization. The description of the "worker" in educational organizations as a "professional" has important implications for the motivating function. The fact that teachers have their own unique need dispositions and that organizations have goals and that the two may not be congruent can be a source of low teacher motivation. The organization must somehow meet the needs of organizational members in the process of achieving organizational goals.

In order to maintain a high level of teacher motivation, teachers must be given an opportunity to participate in decision making and implementing systems which deal with problems of organizational direction, operations, and evaluation. This would ensure teacher sensitivity to and awareness of overall organizational goals. Herzberg, Mausner, and Snyderman found that positive job attitudes are a function of feelings of personal development and self-actualization which are related to achievement, responsibility, work itself, and advancement.[6]

4. *The problem-solving function:* The central theme of the theoretical stance taken in this paper describes human problem solving as the basic process in teacher-pupil systems. Therefore, a basic function of instructional supervisory behavior is to facilitate this process. More specifically the problem-solving function can be described as follows:

a. Facilitation of the processes of goal identification, development of operations for achieving goals, and evaluation of the operations in teacher-pupil systems

b. The development, maintenance, and evaluation of subsystems whose purpose is to impact directly on teacher-pupil systems.

5. *The teacher developing function:* The changing nature of society and changing expectations for the educational institution, expanding knowledge in the organized disciplines, and fast developing educational technology make it imperative that educational organizations provide for the continuous educational development of teachers. This is one of the critical functions of instructional supervisory behavior. An opportunity must be provided for teachers to develop continuously the conceptual, human, and technical skills which are necessary to assure adequate teaching behavior.

[6] Frederick Herzberg, Bernard Mausner, and Barbara B. Snyderman. *The Motivation to Work.* New York: John Wiley & Sons, Inc., 1959. p. 70.

6. *The evaluating function:* Since the educational organization has overall goals which are a function of societal expectations, it is necessary to provide an exacting system for evaluating learning outcomes of the teacher-pupil systems.

References

Max G. Abbott and John T. Lovell, editors. *Change in Perspectives in Educational Administration.* Auburn, Alabama: The School of Education, Auburn University, 1965.

Robert H. Anderson. *Teaching in a World of Change.* New York: Harcourt, Brace & World, Inc., 1966.

Association for Supervision and Curriculum Development. *Learning and the Teacher.* Washington, D.C.: the Association, 1959.

Association for Supervision and Curriculum Development. *Leadership for Improving Instruction.* 1960 Yearbook. Washington, D.C.: the Association, 1960.

Association for Supervision and Curriculum Development. *Perceiving, Behaving, Becoming: A New Focus In Education.* 1962 Yearbook. Washington, D.C.: the Association, 1962.

Association for Supervision and Curriculum Development. *New Insights and the Curriculum.* 1963 Yearbook. Washington, D.C.: the Association, 1963.

Association for Supervision and Curriculum Development. *Individualizing Instruction.* 1964 Yearbook. Washington, D.C.: the Association, 1964.

Association for Supervision and Curriculum Development. *Role of Supervisor and Curriculum Director in a Climate of Change.* 1965 Yearbook. Washington, D.C.: the Association, 1965.

Bernard M. Bass. *Leadership, Psychology, and Organizational Behavior.* New York: Harper & Row Publishers, Inc. 1960.

Warren G. Bennis, Kenneth D. Benne, and Robert Chin, editors. *The Planning of Change.* New York: Holt, Rinehart and Winston, Inc., 1961.

Roald F. Campbell and James M. Lipham, editors. *Administrative Theory as a Guide to Action.* Chicago: Midwest Administration Center, 1960.

Darwin Cartwright and Alvin Zander. *Group Dynamics.* Evanston, Illinois: Row, Peterson and Company, 1960.

Ronald C. Doll. *Curriculum Improvement.* Boston: Allyn and Bacon, Inc., 1964.

Amitai Etzioni. *Complex Organizations.* New York: Holt, Rinehart and Winston, Inc., 1961.

Daniel E. Griffiths. *Human Relations in School Administration.* New York: Appleton-Century-Crofts, Inc., 1956.

Roy R. Grinker, editor. *Toward a Unified Theory of Human Behavior.* New York: Basic Books, Inc., 1956.

Neal Gross and Robert E. Herriott. *Staff Leadership in Public Schools.* New York: John Wiley & Sons, Inc., 1965.

Andrew W. Halpin. *Administrative Theory in Education.* Chicago: Midwest Administration Center, 1958.

Andrew W. Halpin. *Theory and Research in Administration.* New York: The Macmillan Company, 1966.

Ben M. Harris. *Supervisory Behavior in Education.* Englewood Cliffs, New Jersey: Prentice-Hall, Inc., 1963.

Frederick Herzberg, Bernard Mausner, and Barbara B. Snyderman. *The Motivation to Work.* New York: John Wiley & Sons, Inc., 1959.

Earl Kelley and Marie Rasey. *Education and the Nature of Man.* New York: Harper and Brothers, 1952.

Joseph A. Litterer. *Organizations: Structure and Behavior.* New York: John Wiley & Sons, Inc., 1963.

William H. Lucio and John D. McNeil. *Supervision—A Synthesis of Thought and Action.* New York: McGraw-Hill Book Company, Inc., 1962.

James G. March and Herbert A. Simon. *Organizations.* New York: John Wiley & Sons, Inc., 1961.

Matthew B. Miles, editor. *Innovation in Education.* New York: Bureau of Publications, Teachers College, Columbia University, 1964.

Luigi Petrullo and Bernard M. Bass, editors. *Leadership and Interpersonal Behavior.* New York: Holt, Rinehart and Winston, Inc., 1961.

Albert H. Rubenstein and Chadwick J. Haverstroh. *Some Theories of Organization.* Homewood, Illinois: Richard D. Irwin, Inc., and the Dorsey Press, Inc., 1960.

Mildred E. Swearingen. *Supervision of Instruction: Foundations and Dimensions.* Boston: Allyn and Bacon, Inc., 1962.

Ralph W. Tyler. *Basic Principles of Curriculum and Instruction.* Chicago: The University of Chicago Press, 1950.

Kimball Wiles. *Supervision for Better Schools.* Third edition. Englewood Cliffs, New Jersey: Prentice-Hall, Inc., 1967.

Kimball Wiles. *The Changing Curriculum of the American High School* Englewood Cliffs, New Jersey: Prentice-Hall, Inc., 1963.

Supervision as Teaching: An Analogue

Robert H. Anderson

WITHIN the school system and the separate schools that comprise it there are found essentially three categories of persons: (a) the children (or adults) who occupy the role of "learner" and for whose educational benefit the schools are maintained; (b) teachers, supervisors, administrators, and other certified professional workers who are directly or indirectly concerned with the provision of instructional services to the learners; and (c) other adults (secretaries, cafeteria workers, bus drivers, custodians, and so forth) whose work facilitates or supplements the activities of the professional staff but who have no direct responsibility for the achievement of educational goals.

Although it is appropriate to mention that this third group sometimes has a significant effect upon the growth and development of pupils and teachers alike, any contributions that these people may make to the supervision of teachers is essentially an unexpected dividend and it is therefore reasonable to exclude them from our discussion of supervision in action.

In the course of his career the teacher acquires and modifies his teaching repertoire and behavior as a result of numerous forces at work on him and within himself. Probably a substantial fraction of his total teaching personality is more or less self-generated, created as it were out of his own dreams and imagination. Certainly another substantial fraction, especially at the outset of his career, is derived from his long experience as the student of other teachers, from reading books, and magazines and from various general clues (such as movies about school children or teachers) to the way people teach or have taught in the past. Undoubtedly many young teachers consciously or unconsciously imitate the master teachers under whom they served as trainees, and it is probable that the ideas and suggestions gained from course work in educational methods are another component in the overall repertoire with which a new teacher begins.

Once a teacher is on the job, in addition to the self-generated ideas previously mentioned, his teaching pattern is subject to constant modification through contact with pupils, with other teachers, and with various superordinates and consultants. Although it is the latter group to whom this publication is addressed and in whose role(s) we are chiefly interested, it is important to note that both his pupils and his peers have a great influence upon a teacher's work. Furthermore, a strong national trend toward cooperative teaching and a greater tendency to honor and to encourage the critical reactions and suggestions of students make these factors of growing importance in the supervisory environment surrounding the teacher.

At the college level, especially in recent years, the appraisals and the reactions of students to their instructors and to academic programs have become the focus of much discussion and sometimes even of conflict. Newspapers have carried stories about students rallying to the support of popular teachers who are denied faculty tenure, and conversely about students who object to the treatment they are receiving in classrooms. Formal and informal arrangements exist in some colleges for evaluating individual courses and instructors, and sometimes there is provision for direct feedback to the instructors via questionnaires and similar devices. It is difficult to assess the actual effect of such procedures on the instructor's work, but it seems reasonable to assume that they are not usually taken lightly.

Probably more important than official procedures are the various subtle signals and bits of information that instructors note in their day-to-day relationships with students. Evidences of student enthusiasm, of work completed, of high morale, and of a growing commitment to the tasks set down by the faculty will naturally reinforce that faculty in its modus operandi; while signs of disinterest, work slackening, and low morale will probably lead to reexamination of the way things are being done, and even of the goals that are sought. Unfortunately, college instructors rarely receive direct professional assistance (i.e., "supervision") from their deans or department heads, so that sometimes the informal influence system within which student reactions are obtained offers the only outside help a professor receives.

In elementary and secondary schools, perhaps even more than in the colleges, the informal influence system is an important source of insight into the teacher's effectiveness. Furthermore, there is a great deal more information, for example, about each pupil's academic history and tendencies, available to the teacher as he attempts to measure his success with pupils. That sometimes this information is overlooked or neglected, and that too little use is made of supervisors and fellow teachers as additional sources of help, however, seem to be all too true.

The reluctance of some teachers to accept the services of supervisors ✓ may perhaps be explained in part as an aspect of the classic conflict between superordinates and subordinates in the society as a whole. In large part, too, it stems from the inefficacy of many supervisors and in turn from the failure of the profession to develop adequate theories and procedures of supervision. To the latter problem, it is earnestly hoped, current scholarship will address itself with greater energy and clarity.

That teachers within the same school have all too seldom shared pedagogical insights and information, on the other hand, is less the result of role conflicts or ineptitude than it is a consequence of overselling the idea of professional autonomy and of single-teacher responsibility as associated, for example, with the self-contained classroom. By insulating ✓ its members from each other in separate, private teaching spaces, the profession has (perhaps unintentionally) made it unusually difficult for a meaningful professional dialogue to take place within each school.

Over some twenty or thirty years, however, there have emerged in the United States and elsewhere school organization patterns within which teachers work more openly and in collegial partnerships. Ranging all the way from informal collaboration to formally structured teaching teams, these patterns offer (among other things) a greater opportunity for teachers to plan and evaluate together, to see each other at work with children, to exchange ideas and functions, and to interact with each other as professional workers confronting common problems. None of these patterns has yet been developed or evaluated sufficiently to test its ultimate usefulness, but experience already suggests that collegial teaching patterns are here to stay and that they offer a significantly different framework within which the entire subject of teacher supervision, now including the subtopic of "informal supervision by peers," can be examined.

Later in this chapter it will be argued that collegial *supervisory* patterns are a logical next step in the revitalization of the educational professions. First, however, we must take a brief look at supervision as a role not unlike teaching itself.

Supervision and Teaching

"Supervision," a term for which we have long sought a more suitable alternative, ordinarily refers to those things that are done by the appointed officers of a school system to influence (and presumably to stimulate improvement in) the instructional behavior of the teaching staff. Building principals, head teachers, consultants, coordinators, assistant superintendents, directors, supervisors, and similarly-named persons spend anywhere from a small fraction to the great majority of their working time in activities related to the betterment of instruction. Blueprints and models of superior teaching methodology are largely unavailable to these persons, and (perhaps for this reason in particular) sure-fire technologies for working with teachers are equally hard to find. This, in turn, is due in large measure to the relative neglect of theories of instruction, on the one hand, and of theories of supervision on the other.

It is customary to use terms such as "influence," "stimulate," and "inspire" when we talk about the intended impact of a supervisor's work with teachers, much as these terms are often used to describe the teacher's impact on pupils. Words such as "teach" or "instruct" ordinarily bear a somewhat more authoritative meaning, one's mental picture being that of a knowing and controlling adult commanding (though perhaps ever so courteously and gently) the attention of a captive and hopefully cooperative audience. It may be significant that although this image is not par-

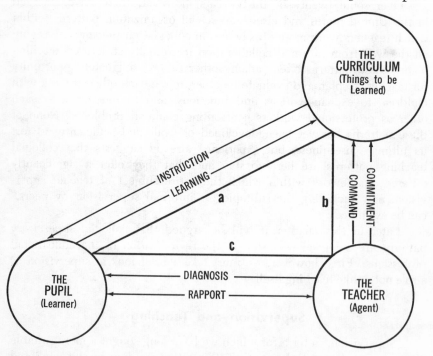

Figure 1. Dimensions of the Teacher's Role

ticularly offensive when the *dramatis personae* are teachers and pupils, it is generally considered inapplicable to the relationship between supervisors and teachers. The profession seems to have been more comfortable with terminology and procedures that suggest a friendly, stimulating relationship between social and intellectual equals, each in a slightly different role but all possessed of those motivations and skills that ensure diligent and effective pursuit of pedagogical excellence.

Without stopping to analyze both the virtues and the dangers inherent in this familiar situation, let us consider an alternative which, though not unfamiliar, needs further development and acceptance. In its essence it conceives of *supervision as the teaching of teachers about teaching.* Its theoretical underpinnings are essentially the same constructs and ideas that undergird teaching itself. In other words, supervisory theory in this case derives from a concept of teaching, and its procedural elements are similar to those which guide teachers in their work with students. The supervisor is seen as a teacher, the dimensions of whose work are virtually the same as those one finds in the work of teachers.

A Conception of the Teacher's Work

In order to illustrate the several dimensions of teaching, though at considerable risk of oversimplification, this author has constructed a triangle showing three elements in relationship to each other.[1] (Page 32.)

In this triangle, horizontal line (c) refers to the relationship between the teacher and the pupil. Basically, this relationship can be broken down into two components, one consisting of all the things that a teacher does in order to diagnose and understand the child and his needs, the other representing the numerous interactions between the child and the teacher which signify and ensure their capacity for working together.

The vertical line (b) in the triangle represents the teacher's relationship to the substance of the school program; that is to say, all of the things (content, personal-social skills, and tools of inquiry and thinking) that the child is expected to learn through his school experience. Again, line (b) has two major components: the teacher's *command* of pertinent knowledge (e.g., Shakespeare's comedies and the process of critical thinking) and the emotional and intellectual *commitment* that he has to the various things he is to teach.

Diagonal line (a), the hypotenuse of the right triangle, also has two major components. When we view it going upwards from left to right,

[1] The following material concerning Figure 1 is adapted from Robert H. Anderson. *Teaching in a World of Change.* New York: Harcourt, Brace & World, Inc., 1966. pp. 14-19.

line (a) represents the learner at work (i.e., "learning"—accepting and reaching out for the knowledge, skills, attitudes, and concepts which constitute the curriculum and its goals). When we view it going down-hill from right to left, it signifies the various activities whereby the teacher strives to cause or enable the child to learn—the insufficient but familiar summary term for these activities being "instruction."

The "compleat" teacher, then, like the compleat angler is possessed of many talents and his professional repertoire includes at least six elements:

1. A command of knowledge (particularly in the field or fields for which he has instructional responsibility but also in other fields as they relate to the field of specialization) and a capacity for its replenishment and expansion

2. Enthusiasm for and commitment to his instructional field(s) manifested in part by a conviction that the things to be taught are im-portant for the learner to possess[2]

3. Command of general information about how children develop, act, think, and feel; plus the capacity to be a skillful clinical observer and diagnostician of each child in his charge

4. The ability to establish an appropriate working relationship, or rapport, with each child and with the class or group as a whole[3] (Line c^2)

5. Thorough understanding of the ways children can and do learn, both in general and within the immediate context

6. Possession of a broad repertoire of pedagogical skills along with the capacity for its replenishment and expansion.

It is possible to summarize these six elements in a simplified triangle as shown in Figure 2 on the following page.

Also reflected in Figure 2 is the fact that schools include a number of pupils with whom teachers deal in aggregates as well as individually. Since teachers often share the teaching responsibility with colleagues,

---

[2] Note that commitment, as defined here, is to the transmission of knowledge to someone else. There are many well-informed people who have great command of knowledge, e.g., scientists working for General Electric or theater critics who know Shakespeare in intimate detail, but theirs is a different form of commitment and they have different ways of using their knowledge to the benefit of others.

[3] Just how far a teacher may legitimately go in establishing a cordial, even affectionate, relationship with the child is an undetermined question. Suffice for purposes of the present discussion that the teacher should demonstrate a sincere interest in the well-being of his pupils, and apply his substantive and pedagogical knowledge to their advantage. Thus, the teacher's behavior elicits the child's *trust* in the teacher's motives, in his professional competency, and in the relevance of his work to the child's own interests. See Anderson, *op. cit.*, pp. 15-16 for elaboration.

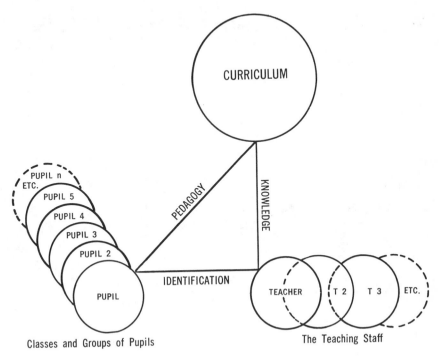

Figure 2

Figure 2 takes note of the cooperative relationships that are possible within the staff.

The Analogue for Supervision

With the triangular representation of the teacher's work as a background concept, let us now approach the work of the supervisor and assess its dimensions by means of the same schema. The reader will recall that we identified supervision as a form of teaching. In Figure 3 (page 36), therefore, we show the supervisor at that corner of the triangle where we earlier showed the teacher.

As can be seen, the teacher is now located in the "student" role, the "things to be learned" (or professional curriculum) including all of the six role elements shown in Figure 1. The supervisor, seen now as an agent who facilitates the efforts of the teacher to learn his craft, becomes responsible for diagnosing and understanding each teacher and his needs with respect to learning-of-craft, and for establishing that sort of relationship with his "student" that will ensure their capacity for working effec-

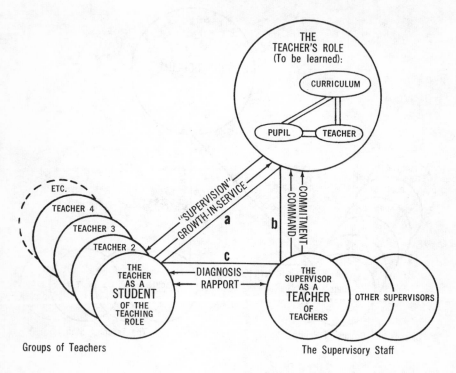

Figure 3. Dimensions of the Supervisor's Role

tively together (see line C). Following the pictorial analogy further, the supervisor is seen as necessarily having both command of all the skills and knowledge which represent effective teaching, and the intellectual and emotional commitment that inspires him to share that property with the teachers he serves (line B). Finally, we see in the hypotenuse (line A) of our new triangle, two familiar components: (a) upwards from left to right, the teacher accepting and reaching out for the additional insight, skills, and knowledge that will make him a more complete and effective craftsman, and (b) downhill from right to left, the various activities whereby the supervisor strives to cause or enable the teacher to learn more about teaching—for which the insufficient but familiar summary term is "supervision."

Though it is unnecessary to describe them here in detail, again we find that there are six elements that comprise the talents and the professional repertoire of the complete supervisor. By clear implication, two of these elements (command of the teaching craft, and zeal for its propagation) call for the supervisor to have extraordinary insight into the teaching role. Two of them call for an understanding of ways that teachers actually do learn and change, and for a broad repertoire of (pedagogical) skills and techniques of the sort that can facilitate such change behavior within the teaching staff. Two of them call for talent and training in studying and dealing with teachers as learners; it is essential to earn the teacher's *trust* in one's motives and competence.

In Figure 3, also, is reflected the fact that teachers come in multiples and supervisors frequently deal with them in groups. Since supervisors sometimes share the supervisory responsibility with colleagues, Figure 3 also takes note of the cooperative relationships that are possible within the administrative-supervisory staff.

The reader may already have noticed that it is possible to extend our analogy one step further by creating an additional figure in which the *supervisor* is shown as the student of his supervisory craft, and in which professors, superintendents, assistant superintendents, and others carry the responsibility for overseeing and training supervisory personnel. See Figure 4, which shows this possibility in abbreviated form.

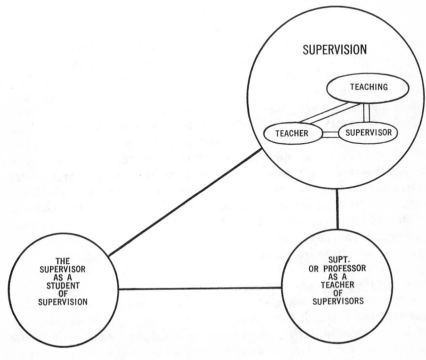

Figure 4

The Analogue: A Discussion

There may be some to whom the definition of supervision as teaching is either unfamiliar or objectionable. Admittedly, it seems at first glance to be somewhat inconsistent with the notion of supervisors and teachers as fellow professionals with equal dignity and self-respect. However, there is no reason to abhor or resist a relationship among adults in which there is assumed a higher degree of knowledge or skill on the part of one person, any more than it is degrading to a child because his teacher has more knowledge and experience in the academic world than he. At its best, the relationship between a child and his teacher is productive and satisfying and there is no loss of dignity because the child is in some ways dependent upon his teacher. At its best, too, that relationship is marked by the child's confidence that his teacher labors effectively in his best interest. An achievement by the child is gratifying both to him and to his teacher, and the child's growing independence of adult assistance is both a mutual goal and a source of mutual pride as it occurs.

At its best, then, the relationship between the teacher whose learning consists of increasing his pedagogical craftsmanship and the person (i.e., supervisor) who serves as *his* teacher can and should resemble the pupil-teacher relationship we have just described. Granted that the teacher's dependency upon the supervisor takes more subtle forms than does the child's dependency, and granted, too, that a relationship among mature adults is necessarily different in important ways from an adult-child relationship, it is nevertheless useful to pursue the analogy and to argue that supervisors should define their role as a high-level form of teaching.

Many supervisors fail to adjust to their supervisory roles, perhaps in part because they have been unwilling or unable to make the emotional and intellectual adjustments that are required. Some continue to regard themselves primarily as teachers of children, and they find greater satisfaction in their occasional opportunities to work again with children— e.g., while teaching a demonstration lesson or taking over the classroom of an absent teacher—than they find in their work with adults. Most supervisors have received too little preparation for their role, and all too few have been helped to see that there are rich satisfactions to be gained from teaching and working with adults. Some feel isolated and lonely in their new role, cut off, as it were, from the once-familiar social life in the teachers' lounge and in the faculty bridge clubs (or poker games). Sometimes it takes many years for newly appointed principals and supervisors to establish friendships of equal significance with fellow supervisors, and to wean themselves, in a sense, of the old satisfactions gained through teacher-to-pupil and teacher-to-teacher interaction.

Happier and more effective, indeed, will be the supervisor who recognizes and accepts the different ground rules that govern a supervisor's personal and professional life. This implies, as does Figure 3, that he must acquire an understanding of classroom teaching that goes far beyond his own personal repertoire when he was a teacher. He must observe a great variety of teaching performances in the school or schools he serves, and arrive at a deeper understanding of all the many ways that teachers deal with and diagnose children, approach the curriculum, arrange pupil groupings, and allocate resources.

He must study each teacher with at least the same care he once invested in his most interesting and/or problematical pupils, probing for the best ways of "getting to" that teacher and developing, in the process, an array of devices for releasing and increasing the pedagogical powers that reside in his staff, both individually and collectively. He must learn how to read the signs of his successes and his failures; how to appreciate, for example, the significance of a classroom door (formerly resolutely closed) left open or a teacher's new awareness of a colleague's skill with small groups. He must learn to accept, too, the legitimate remoteness of his position when circumstances so require, learning how to find comradeship and solace within the supervisory group just as teachers are frequently forced to accept the gulf that inevitably separates them from the world of children.

Success in supervision, then, rests in large measure upon the supervisor's ability to define and accept his role as having essentially the same dimensions as that of the teacher, but with a more mature and challenging clientele and with pedagogy itself as the focus of all intellectual endeavor. So defined, the supervisor's work is scarcely for pedagogical amateurs or for flabby spirits. It requires far more preparation and orientation than has usually been provided, and it deserves more attention and support from the school superintendency than it ordinarily receives.

Cooperative Supervision

Before concluding this chapter on supervision as teaching, let us draw one final lesson for supervision from the teaching profession and the direction in which teaching seems to be heading. Earlier were mentioned the strong trend toward patterns of teacher collaboration and the potential benefits that may accrue to teachers as a result of such collaboration. We now turn to the potential advantages of collegial supervision, a topic which has recently received attention in the literature and which seems capable of breathing new health and life into an overburdened role.[4]

Among the reasons for the emergence of cooperative teaching patterns have been (a) the increasing difficulty, in view of the vast increase in knowledge, of any one teacher maintaining adequate control of instructional technology and of the content(s) for which he is responsible; (b) correspondingly, a trend toward greater specialization within teaching; (c) concern for the integration of the separate subject areas, which is difficult in schools that are merely departmentalized; (d) a desire for greater flexibility in the grouping and subgrouping of pupils, in the utilization of staff and material resources, and in scheduling and use of space; (e) the search for ways to break down the rigidity of conventional graded structure; (f) a realization that no one teacher's personality and teaching style can be equally appropriate to meet the varying needs of all his pupils; (g) efforts to find more flexible ways to train and induct newcomers to the teaching profession; (h) efforts to include part-time teachers and nonprofessionals in the work force of the school; and (i) the recognized need for more professional dialogue within the staff. There are probably other reasons, and some of the ones mentioned may be disputed by some readers, but let us take a moment to examine these same categories within the context of our analogue.

If cooperative staff organization is appropriate and necessary in ensuring flexibility and efficiency among teachers, it may be equally appropriate in ensuring flexibility and efficiency among supervisors. Consider, for a moment, nine arguments that might be offered:

1. It becomes increasingly difficult, as pedagogical knowledge expands, for any one supervisor to maintain adequate control of supervision as a field, and of content area(s);

2. Correspondingly, there needs to be greater specialization within supervision (e.g., one supervisor a specialist in working with inexperienced teachers, another a media specialist, another to keep up with new math and science trends);

---

[4] (a) Nicholas Anastasiow and Abraham S. Fischler. "A Proposal for Teaming Principals." *The National Elementary Principal* 44:59-64; November 1964.

(b) Anderson, *op. cit.*, pp. 125-27.

(c) Morris L. Cogan. "Clinical Supervision by Groups." *The College Supervisor.* 43rd Yearbook, The Association for Student Teaching. Dubuque, Iowa: William C. Brown, 1964. pp. 114-31.

(d) James Greig and Robert R. Lee. "Cooperative Administration." *The National Elementary Principal* 44:71-76; January 1965.

(e) Maurice E. St. Mary. "The Administrative Team in Supervision." *The National Elementary Principal* 45:59-61; April 1966.

3. Supervisors of separate content areas can work together to ensure an integrated program, especially with respect to the identification of common goals;

4. A cooperative arrangement offers more flexibility in the use of supervisory resources;

5. A cooperative arrangement would make it easier to cope with the differential needs and growth potentiality of the various staff members;

6. No one supervisor can "be all things to all the people" he serves;

7. Newcomers to the supervisory role could be inducted into their roles more easily with the help of veteran colleagues;

8. Part-time supervisors and various semi-supervisory colleagues can easily be included in a cooperative group; and

9. Supervisors no less than teachers have a great need for continuous professional dialogue.

To these arguments might be added that experience has shown that teachers react favorably to supervision by groups of supervisors, since group supervision tends to reduce some of the factors (such as bias, or incompetence on the part of an individual supervisor) to which teachers sometimes object when they are visited only by one person.

In Figure 3, therefore, the supervisory staff was shown as a group, just as the teaching staff was shown as a group in Figure 2. It is hoped that the analogy, carried thus to its logical extreme, is one with which the supervisory profession will feel increasingly comfortable.

In summary, supervision and teaching may be seen as roles with many of the same dimensions, and hence with similar problems and similar satisfactions. Particularly when supervisors join forces in carrying out their collective responsibilities toward teachers, it is argued that the problems become more manageable and the role satisfactions are accordingly increased. Within the framework of cooperative supervision, each supervisor finds a source of ideas and strength, a clearer view of the many ways whereby teachers can be helped to grow, and significant opportunities for his own professional growth-in-service. Obviously these benefits will not accrue automatically, just as they do not accrue to classroom teachers without earnest effort, but for the zealous and professionally minded supervisor the analogue of supervision as a teaching role seems to offer a wholesome and promising perspective.

Implications for Educational Practice

John D. Greene

SUPERVISORY effort must have purpose, and yet must recognize that outcomes will vary with situations. The application of a supervision theory requires that goals be modified as insight is gained during various operational and developmental stages in instructional programs. Generally, the purpose, goals, and objectives of any applied theory of supervision should be compatible with what is known about fostering the full development of individuals to accord with sound principles of human learning and in keeping with values crucial to our way of life.

Values and Purpose

From what source do we obtain the purpose that gives us perspective and direction and serves as a basis for supervisory behavior? The needs of society are one obvious source. Yet, do we know the needs of our present day complex society? A century ago, when life was more simple, our physical, social, economic, and self-needs were determined in a more direct and less complex fashion, and the educational purpose relating to societal needs was easily distinguishable. Today's world is different; schools endeavor to serve all the children of all the people from the highly disadvantaged to the highly affluent in a technological and scientific setting.

Henry Adams in 1905 projected our thinking when he said, "Every American who lived in the year 2000 would know how to control unlimited power. He would think in complexities unimaginable to an earlier mind." We are not having to wait until the year 2000 to witness Henry Adams' prediction; the salient signs of the 'sixties force us to recognize that our confrontation is now, and that clearly stated goals or purpose in terms of present and future educational needs are imperative.

Historically, endeavors to state educational purpose include such statements as that of the President's Commission on Higher Education in 1947:

The first goal in education for democracy is the full, rounded, and continuing development of the person. The discovery, training, and utilization of individual talents is of fundamental importance in a free society. To liberate and perfect the intrinsic powers of every citizen is the central purpose of democracy, and its furtherance of individual self-realization is its greatest glory.

We probably would accept the terminology and the broad intent of this purpose, but the more significant problem is implementation—action directed toward the attainment of applicable and testable goals and purposes.

Values that have stood the test of time should not quell the possibility of finding and accepting new values as they emerge in the process of human interaction during this era of accelerated change. Regardless of the accepted values that undergird supervisory behavior, the central purpose of education and supervision should always be in focus. A statement to this effect was made by the Educational Policies Commission:

Among the many important purposes of American schools the fostering of the development of individual freedom and effectiveness and the progress of the society require the development of every citizen's rational powers. . . . Man has before him the possibility of a new level of greatness, a new realization of human dignity and effectiveness. The instrument which will realize this possibility is that kind of education which frees the mind and enables it to contribute to a full and worthy life.[1]

Supervisory behavior must have purpose which in turn gives practitioners needed perspective and clarity of direction in place of uncertain, floundering, nonpurposeful, nonproductive effort.

Clarification of Purpose

In most school systems throughout the nation various persons have assumed supervisory responsibility. The ASCD 1965 Yearbook, *The Role of Supervisor and Curriculum Director in a Climate of Change*,[2] makes no attempt to give titles to all the persons with supervisory responsibility. Instead, the yearbook committee used the term in the broadest sense to

[1] The Educational Policies Commission. *The Central Purpose of Education.* Washington, D.C.: National Education Association—American Association of School Administrators, 1961.

[2] The Association for Supervision and Curriculum Development. *The Role of Supervisor and Curriculum Director in a Climate of Change.* 1965 Yearbook. Robert R. Leeper, editor. Washington, D.C.: the Association, 1965.

indicate persons such as consultants, special and/or general supervisors, curriculum leaders, or any person in an instructional leadership role who contributes to the improvement of teaching and/or the implementation and development of curriculum. The authors of the sections in this present booklet include superintendents, directors, supervisors, principals, consultants, and helping or head teachers when referring to supervisory personnel.

Regardless of the assigned supervisory title from the table of organization, it is not impossible for these persons unknowingly to work at cross purposes. It is assumed that greater productivity would result if commonality of purpose were established and accepted by supervisory staff members. Teachers who profit most directly from supervisory effort are more likely to obtain, accept, and assimilate supervisory assistance if those who are endeavoring to render assistance perceive commonality of goals. Supervisors may be unaware of their operational incongruencies; while fully aware of their personal bias and operational differences. Invariably this is due to personal needs and goals that obscure or counterbalance the overall purpose of schooling. Unfortunately the unsuspecting teacher, the one-who-is-supposed-to-profit, is caught in the crossfire of inconsistencies from the supposed-to-be-supervisory helpers. Clarification of purpose is not necessarily accomplished by administrative edict, but by identifying and working on a common concern that looms larger than the existing differences. The following example may illustrate:

A new director of instruction was charged specifically with coordinating the efforts of a staff of 18 supervisors and consultants of a central office staff. in quasi-visionary terms, a philosophical statement of purpose used such terminology as the following:

"The overall goal of the supervisors is to work with others, specifically teachers, in such ways that in the final analysis the students of those teachers will become more self-realized individuals in keeping with each student's aptitudes, abilities, and aspirations in life so long as each person's self-realization is compatible with our democratic way of life."

Each of the 18 supervisors was to analyze his own actions in relation to his own positive influence on teachers under his jurisdiction. A more specific objective became, "How do you work with teachers who have a direct impact on the development of students in such ways that the teachers' understanding and competency are continually improved?" Each supervisor developed his individual program of assistance to teachers adhering only to his own area of specialization. Each had developed an effective program when viewed individually; however, there was a lack of coordination among the supervisors.

Effort was made at the beginning of the school year by the new director to bring the instructional supervisors together into a supervisory working team, yet individuality was to be recognized and nourished. Individual supervisors did not recognize the lack of unity and how this could affect the overall productivity of the instructional program. The new director did not pointedly refer to the discrepancy—instead he perceived there was a lack of unified effort because there had not been opportunities for teachers to work together as a group, selecting common problems that were larger than the existing differences (and in the process of solving the common problem developing a greater understanding and respect for each other and becoming a compatible team).

After several informal efforts were made by the new director of instruction to develop the knowledge, skills, and attitudes requisite for facilitating learning, the special consultants and the general supervisors agreed that this topic should be pursued by the group as a whole and that general ground rules should be established as follows:

1. The group would hold regular staff consultations.

2. Objective recorded information would be presented by each supervisor as long as it related to the topic of facilitating learning. (Most of the data shared were everyday experiences in which the supervisor helped the teacher. In time, as the group developed more acceptance, they shared objective accounts in which they admittedly hindered the learning process.)

3. General action research methodology would be used. (At times there were attempts to be more scientific, by developing and testing hypotheses.)

4. In evaluation, the objective recorded data of each supervisor would be used as well as the recorder's notes from each meeting, plus less formal means of detecting how greater supervisor competency had been reached in helping teachers understand and facilitate the learning process with students.

In time the new director and the central office supervisors could sense the development of team effort as each supervisor saw not only his own role in facilitating learning but his relation to the work of supervisors in other academic disciplines. Unsurprisingly the new director became more adequate in his leadership responsibility during the process of developing greater staff supervisory competency.

In an earlier section, Lucio refers to goals and purposes from the viewpoint of the Revisionists, so named in an attempt to reconcile the Scientific Management philosophy with that of the Human Relationists. The Revisionists believe the "individual goals and the organizational goals must be fused through commitment and leadership activity." Likewise, when teachers and supervisors are committed to "what-is-best-for-students" their individual goals and subsequent action are directed toward accomplishing that purpose. Supervisory purpose is echoed by supervisory behavior, defined by Lovell's definition, as follows:

Instructional supervisory behavior is officially designated organizational behavior which is external to the teacher-pupil system but is calculated to impact directly and purposefully in such a way as to facilitate student learning.

Characteristics of Supervisory Personnel

In addition to clarification of purpose, those persons who are charged with implementation of supervision must display competence if they are to increase competency in teachers. Notwithstanding the fact that each person in a supervisory role is an individual, as unique as his fingerprints, the focus must be on some common characteristics of scholarship regardless of title and individuality. Lucio has cautioned that attention to human relations alone is not enough; yet, a supervisor who is endeavoring to help a teacher or principal become more competent should be basically oriented to and accepting of human beings.

Psychologically, some degree of self-acceptance is a prerequisite to identification with and acceptance of others. However, acceptance of self and others should not be interpreted as self-satisfaction or complacency. Intrinsic satisfactions are gained from seeing efforts reflected through the modified and improved instructional behavior of teachers.

The competent supervisor who has the assigned task of implementing specified organizational goals displays personal qualities such as:

1. *Intelligence*—with full realization that intelligence is not a static human quality and that human beings possess a variety and range of intellectual abilities, it still remains there is no substitute for operational intelligence.

2. *Questing quotient*—the supervisor is forever learning, and he possesses a high motivational eagerness for more knowledge and ways of applying it in schools.

3. *Coping ability*—he adjusts to the demands of a rapidly changing society. The new, ever-changing societal demands become a challenge, not a threat.

4. *Faith in self*—he believes in himself and others; he believes in the dignity and worth of man and that every person is motivated to do something, to become.

In the ASCD 1962 Yearbook, *Perceiving, Behaving, Becoming: A New Focus In Education*, Carl R. Rogers [3] alludes to appropriate characteristics of supervisors:

. . . . the adjectives which seem more generally fitting are adjectives such as enriching, exciting, rewarding, challenging, meaningful. This process of healthy living is not, I am convinced, a life for the fainthearted. It involves the

---

[3] Carl R. Rogers. "Toward Becoming a Fully Functioning Person." In: *Perceiving, Behaving, Becoming: A New Focus For Education*. 1962 Yearbook. Arthur W. Combs, chairman. Washington, D.C.: Association for Supervision and Curriculum Development, 1962. p. 32.

stretching and growing of becoming more and more of one's potentialities. It involves the courage to be. It means launching oneself fully into the stream of life. Yet the deeply exciting thing about human beings is that when the individual is inwardly free, he chooses this process of becoming.

Earl C. Kelley's statements in the ASCD 1962 Yearbook characterize effective supervisory functions in referring to the perceptions of a fully functioning person:

He must see in his experiential background some history of success. He needs to see process, the building and becoming nature of himself. This being so, he will see that today has no meaning in the absence of yesterdays and tomorrows. In fact, there could be no today except for both yesterday and tomorrow. He must like what he sees, at least well enough for it to be operational.[4]

Certainly today's supervisor has a task that is more demanding than ever in the history of educational supervision. His work is characterized by a variety of tasks, diverse human relationships involving peers, superordinates, and subordinates plus a range of procedural problems, nebulous goals, and a lack of evaluative instruments to measure the significant aspects of his influence on teacher learning. If he does not have a clear perspective of his tasks, his objectives and, direction, it follows that the present pressures of the public and the intensified conflicting demands of an uncertain anxious society will cause the inadequate educational leader to flounder and be ineffectual. In contrast, the highly motivated and competent educational leader will assess the reality of the situation, identify problems, plan his strategy, and perceive his task as an exciting challenge.

Climate and Strategy

Effective supervisors are educational change agents, and their effectiveness is contingent on their sensitivity to the existing operational climate as well as an awareness of strategies involving change. In reality, educational innovations and new information confront the supervisor and before he can understandably assess, much less implement, those innovations he must intellectually grasp their significance.

Factors to be considered as an integral part of the setting in which supervisors work are such variables as: (a) affluent socioeconomic areas juxtaposed to poverty pockets in the same or separate school systems; (b) problems and complexities of school desegregation and integration;

---

[4] Earl C. Kelley. "The Fully Functioning Self." In: *Perceiving, Behaving, Becoming: A New Focus For Education.* 1962 Yearbook. Arthur W. Combs, chairman. Washington, D.C.: Association for Supervision and Curriculum Development, 1962. p. 10.

(c) modern curricular developments with graduated degrees of soundness; (d) the knowledge explosion; (e) impact of technology and subsequent commercial pressures; and (f) federal financing and proposals for national assessment. Since schools, in most communities, have become the largest business enterprise, it is understandable that many external pressures befall the educational establishment from taxpayers, vendors, and parent expectations; yet these external forces do not preclude the impetus of internal pressures and demands that are self-imposed by the sensitive, dedicated educational leader. The way the supervisor perceives his operational setting is likely to determine his supervisory behavior.

Professional Faculty Study—A Strategy Example

Based upon the belief that the single school is the most strategic unit for educational change, given supportive conditions, one general supervisor and the school's supervising principal proposed and entitled their strategy, "Professional Faculty Study." [5] This faculty group of 22 elementary teachers (K-6), including principal and supervisor, organized their study with focus on the child and the curriculum. The supervisor and principal became participating learning members with the faculty as well as serving in a guiding role. Their organizational procedure included 12 meetings appropriately spaced throughout the school year. For methodology they adhered to the following points:

1. Begin with a teaching concern; that is, the individual teacher identifies a teaching problem about which he needs more information so that he can improve his own competency.

2. A student is selected who represents the teaching concern; for example, several sixth-grade boys do not read on sixth-grade level. Jack is one of these boys. Thus, he is selected for more careful study, as he represents this teacher's concern in the area of reading. (Although the example used here is reading, participants in study groups could select students who represent a wide range of concerns including: Science, Word Attack, Discipline, Criteria for Promotion and Retention, Readiness for Different Learning Activities, Pressures on the Child, Motivation, The Superior Student, The Underachiever, Learning Modern Math, Creativity, Fostering Inquiry, or Following a Selected Child in a Nongraded Situation or in a Team Teaching Experiment.)

3. The curricular concern identified by the teacher and the student(s) is presented to the faculty study group by the second meeting.

4. An early effort is made by the teacher, principal, and/or supervisor

[5] John I. Goodlad. "The Individual School and Its Principal: Key Setting and Key Person in Educational Leadership." *Educational Leadership* 13(1): 2-6; October 1955.

collecting the data to specify what he definitely knows at the time about the student and the teaching concern he represents. For example, if the teaching concern pertains to "poor readers," the first step is to indicate what he already knows about the causes; then indicate the things he does not know, and then indicate the things that should be known about "poor readers" in order to improve the student's ability to read. These data are secured from many sources and shared during the professional faculty meetings.

5. Faculty members make their best guesses as to why the problem exists and list causal hypotheses. For example: What are the possible reasons (hypotheses) for Jack's not reading on sixth-grade level?

6. From available sources of information, data are collected that will validate or invalidate the hypotheses proposed.

7. The validated hypotheses become the basis for tryouts in the classroom; thus, a real test is given in the classroom situation.

8. If there is evidence to show that the validated hypotheses work in the tryouts in the classroom, then some generalizations applicable in other similar school situations can be drawn.

Evaluation of the professional faculty study in this example was continuous and a significant factor in the operational procedures.

The following points were stressed in the periodic evaluation of the professional faculty study:

1. Is the problem under study of real and significant concern to the members?

2. Does each faculty participant follow some organized methodology in working on the teaching concern?

3. Are representatives of the faculty participating in the planning of each meeting?

4. Are the principal and supervisor actively involved in planning meetings?

5. Is adequate time provided for each meeting? (60-90 minutes)

6. Is the professional study free from administrative announcements and detail?

7. Is the physical setting appropriate for a study of this type?

8. Is there a relaxed atmosphere in which to work?

9. Do members feel free to participate?

10. Do faculty members have a sense of professional pride in the study?

11. Is a systematic effort made to evaluate the study?

12. Are the understandings and skills obtained in the study being used by individual teachers in the classrooms?

13. What insights have the principal and the supervisor internalized from the study that will make them more competent as leaders? (Has their supervisory behavior been modified and improved?)

Evaluation of this professional faculty study was generally positive and their suggestions for improvement were incorporated by several other faculties working in a similarly organized manner for the purpose of improving their competency. The faculty study group is one (not the only) vehicle at the "grass roots level" in which faculty members have an opportunity to work together on common problems, with the principal and/or supervisor serving in a guiding as well as participating role. A summary statement by one teacher in this study indicated realization that growth takes place in the ever-questing process:

> Although we study, we minister, we strive
> But as complete teachers do we ever arrive?

Evaluation of the Supervisory Function

The reasons why supervisory behavior proves to be effective are many, complex, and interrelated. Lack of effective teacher behavior is oftentimes evaluated as the reason for inadequate results. However, it is rare for those who are charged with the supervisory function to be evaluated. Granted, the supervisor when selected was thought to be adequate and to possess skills appropriate for the time. Yet in this era of change has the supervisor kept pace? Does the supervisor engage in a periodic refueling and "retreading" process? Should not the evaluative spotlight be turned on the supervisor if evaluation of the teacher is accepted practice?

Some of the techniques used in evaluating teacher behavior may have implications for judging the effectiveness of supervisors. Such instruments may include video tapes or recordings. The use of a third person in the supervisor-teacher setting, to analyze, provide insight, and evaluate the dynamics of the supervisory function may be tried. However, a prerequisite to supervisory evaluation is the necessity for a more precise delineation and identification of supervisory purpose and function as well as evaluative instruments to assess what is purported to be important to the function.

Future Supervisory Behavior

While no accurate crystal ball is at hand to predict what the supervisory function may be, there is some basis for speculation that in a climate of change the function will be different. The individual supervisor "peddling his product" to the exclusion of others may in the not-too-distant future become a member of a supervisory team working for the good of teachers—not too different from a team of teachers working for the good of students. It is possible that a supervisory team approach could provide opportunity for: (a) clarifying common purpose, (b) capitalizing on strengths, (c) using collegial interaction and dialogue, (d) providing immediate evaluative feedback, and (e) developing greater self-awareness. Observations of those persons who currently work as individual supervisors reveal that each supervisor seeks consultation, dialogue, or reflection from a colleague who serves as a "sounding-board." The supervisory team approach could provide the means of satisfying this need more systematically.

Spears, an advocate of other promising supervisory practices, says:

A superintendent of schools should acknowledge and accept responsibility for the primary purpose of his being, which is leadership in providing the best instruction for his students.[6]

One superintendent in a school system of 70,000 students who faced up to his responsibilities (in accordance with Spears' suggestion) scheduled one day in each week for the specific task of improving instruction. On the specified day he, the superintendent, essentially became team leader of selected central office instructional staff members to visit schools, using the following operational procedure:

1. The superintendent and instructional team members visited a particular school and met with the principal and the principal's leadership members (having previously arranged for and indicated the purpose of the proposed visit).

2. The principal, in a discussion section, was asked to give the purpose of the school as well as indicate his objectives as key person in the school.

3. The principal and his school leadership staff were asked to indicate candidly the strengths and weaknesses of their school program and in turn the superintendent's team responded with objective evaluations of strengths and weaknesses of the school's instructional program.

Teachers and administrators reacted favorably to the initial and follow-up work. Evaluative statements included: "Someone cares"; "We're able to voice our teaching concerns"; "We secure help that enables me to be a better teacher"; "I get needed materials"; "I have more respect for my principal"; and, "I've learned that they have some helpful, capable people on the central office staff." An experienced principal remarked, "I've been a teacher or principal for almost 40 years and it is the first time that any superintendent put first things first."

In summary:

[6] Harold Spears, Superintendent of San Francisco Unified Schools and President of AASA, in a speech to Alabama School Administrators, Mobile, Alabama, October 30, 1966.

1. The superintendent recognized his chief responsibility as instructional leader and acted accordingly (no easy task in a system of over 3,000 teachers, principals, and supervisors, and 70,000 students).

2. The superintendent, by virtue of his position, could "quarterback" the team of members from the central office and school, yet delegate responsibility to team members.

3. Teachers, principals, and supervisors were generally open to suggestions.

4. Support from the school board, desire for continuous improvement by the community, support of key persons, both lay and professional, were factors in the program.

Sources for Future Supervisory Systems

The reports of Lucio and Lovell have described models for supervisory systems based on extrapolations from theory in human relations, group dynamics, behavioral sciences, as well as industry and institutional management. Certainly the various new organizational arrangements now appearing as well as new technological assets will have an effect on future supervisory systems, for example, the computerized storage and retrieval of data and such developments as the Educational Development Laboratories, Research and Development Centers, and other organizations.

The League of Cooperating Schools recently organized in Southern California represents a tripartite agreement for educational change among 19 school districts in Southern California, the University of California at Los Angeles, and the Institute for Development of Educational Activities (IDEA). According to the director, John I. Goodlad, the following structure has been established: (a) each district has assigned a single elementary or middle school to the League; (b) UCLA has committed its laboratory school and certain resources of the UCLA School of Education's research and development center, whose function is the development of criteria and techniques for evaluating instructional programs; and (c) IDEA, through its research and development division, has committed financial, administrative, and consultative support and, through its innovation-demonstration and information divisions, a network for disseminating findings and promising practices.

The formation of the League of Cooperating Schools may serve to initiate innovations in the representative schools of the 19 districts which in time will affect not only the schools in Southern California but also others throughout the United States. Information helpful in future educational supervisory endeavors may result from this unified approach to improved schooling.